Bags a
Backpa

Luxurious Aran/Celtic stitch patterns enrich the look of 8 crochet bags, backpacks, and tablet covers by Bonnie Barker.

LEISURE ARTS, INC.
Maumelle, Arkansas

Cabled Handbag

INTERMEDIATE

Finished Size: 10" wide x 10¼" deep (25.5 cm x 26 cm)
(excluding Handle Casing and Handles)

SHOPPING LIST

Yarn (Medium Weight) MEDIUM 4

[5 ounces, 251 yards
(142 grams, 230 meters) per skein]:

- ☐ Dk Green - 1 skein
- ☐ Lt Green - 1 skein

Crochet Hook

- ☐ Size I (5.5 mm)
  or size needed for gauge

Additional Supplies

- ☐ 8$^1/_8$" x 4" (20.5 cm x 10 cm) pair of Handles
- ☐ Yarn needle
- ☐ ½ yard (.5 meter) Fabric for lining (recommended)
- ☐ Sewing needle
- ☐ Matching thread

GAUGE INFORMATION

In Body pattern,

16 sts and 8 rnds/rows = 4" (10 cm)

Gauge Swatch: 4" (10 cm) square

With Lt Green, ch 17.

Row 1: Dc in third ch from hook **(2 skipped chs count as first dc)** and in each ch across: 16 dc.

Row 2: Ch 2 **(counts as first dc)**, turn; work BPdc around next st *(Fig. 3, page 46)* and each st across to last dc, dc in last dc.

Row 3: Ch 2 **(counts as first dc)**, turn; work FPdc around next BPdc and each BPdc across to last dc, dc in last dc.

Rows 4-8: Repeat Rows 2 and 3 twice; then repeat Row 2 once **more**.

Finish off.

STITCH GUIDE

BACK POST DOUBLE CROCHET *(abbreviated BPdc)*

YO, insert hook from **back** to **front** around post of st indicated ***(Fig. 3, page 46)***, YO and pull up a loop (3 loops on hook), (YO and draw through 2 loops on hook) twice.

FRONT POST DOUBLE CROCHET *(abbreviated FPdc)*

YO, insert hook from **front** to **back** around post of st indicated ***(Fig. 3, page 46)***, YO and pull up a loop (3 loops on hook), (YO and draw through 2 loops on hook) twice.

FRONT POST TREBLE CROCHET *(abbreviated FPtr)*

YO twice, insert hook from **front** to **back** around post of st indicated ***(Fig. 3, page 46)***, YO and pull up a loop (4 loops on hook), (YO and draw through 2 loops on hook) 3 times.

INSTRUCTIONS
Body

With Dk Green, ch 40.

Rnd 1: Dc in third ch from hook **(2 skipped chs do not count as a st)** and in each ch across to last ch, 4 dc in last ch; working in free loops of beginning ch *(Fig. 2b, page 46)*, dc in next ch and in each ch across to same ch as first dc, 3 dc in same ch; join with slip st to first dc: 80 dc.

Rnd 2 (Right side)**:** Ch 2 **(does not count as a st, now and throughout Body)**, turn; ★ skip next 2 dc, work FPtr around next 2 dc, working in **front** of FPtr just made, work FPtr around 2 skipped dc; repeat from ★ around; join with slip st to first FPtr: 20 Cables.

Note: Loop a short piece of yarn around any stitch to mark Rnd 2 as **right** side.

Rnd 3: Ch 2, turn; work BPdc around next FPtr and each FPtr around; join with slip st to first BPdc: 80 BPdc.

Rnd 4: Ch 2, turn; ★ skip next 2 BPdc, work FPtr around next 2 BPdc, working in **front** of FPtr just made, work FPtr around 2 skipped BPdc; repeat from ★ around; join with slip st to first FPtr changing to Lt Green *(Fig. A)*, cut Dk Green.

Fig. A

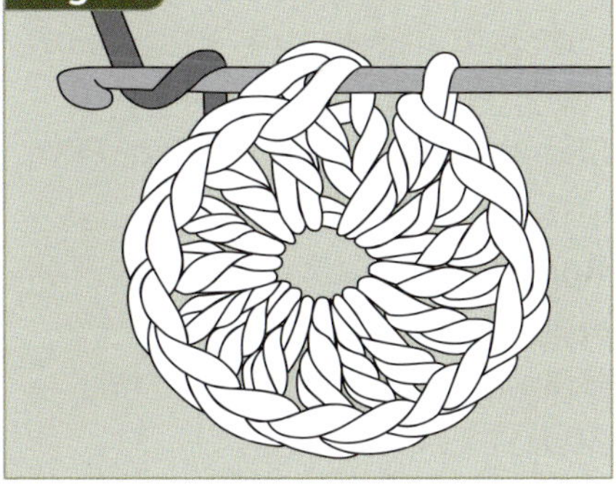

Rnd 5: Ch 2, turn; work BPdc around next FPtr and each FPtr around; join with slip st to first BPdc.

Rnd 6: Ch 3 **(does not count as a st, now and throughout)**, turn; skip next 4 BPdc, work FPtr around next 2 BPdc, working in **front** of FPtr just made, work FPtr around third and fourth skipped BPdc, ★ skip next 2 BPdc, work FPtr around next 2 BPdc, working in **front** of FPtr just made, work FPtr around 2 skipped BPdc; repeat from ★ around ending by working around first 2 skipped BPdc; join with slip st to first FPtr.

Rnd 7: Ch 2, turn; work BPdc around next FPtr and each FPtr around; join with slip st to first BPdc.

Rnd 8: Ch 2, turn; ★ skip next 2 BPdc, work FPtr around next 2 BPdc, working in **front** of FPtr just made, work FPtr around 2 skipped BPdc; repeat from ★ around; join with slip st to first FPtr changing to Dk Green, cut Lt Green.

Rnds 9 and 10: Repeat Rnds 5 and 6.

Rnds 11 and 12: Repeat Rnds 3 and 4.

Rnds 13-19: Repeat Rnds 5-11.

Rnd 20: Ch 2, turn; ★ skip next 2 BPdc, work FPtr around next 2 BPdc, working in **front** of FPtr just made, work FPtr around 2 skipped BPdc; repeat from ★ around; join with slip st to first FPtr.

Rnd 21: Ch 1, do **not** turn; sc in first 8 FPtr, work FPdc around next 24 FPtr, sc in next 16 FPtr, work FPdc around next 24 FPtr, sc in last 8 FPtr; join with slip st to first sc, finish off.

Handle Casing
FIRST SIDE

Row 1: With **right** side facing, skip first 7 sc on Rnd 21 and join Dk Green with slip st in next sc; ch 2 **(counts as first dc, now and throughout)**, work FPdc around next 24 FPdc, dc in next sc, leave remaining sts unworked: 26 sts.

Row 2: Ch 2, turn; work BPdc around next 24 FPdc, dc in last dc.

Row 3: Ch 2, turn; work FPdc around next 24 BPdc, dc in last dc.

Rows 4-6: Repeat Rows 2 and 3 once, then repeat Row 2 once **more**; at end of Row 6, finish off leaving 20" (51 cm) strand for sewing Handle Casing.

SECOND SIDE

Row 1: With **right** side facing, skip next 14 sc from First Side and join Dk Green with slip st in next sc; ch 2, work FPdc around next 24 FPdc, dc in next sc, leave remaining sts unworked: 26 sts.

Rows 2-6: Work same as First Side.

Thread yarn needle with long end from either Handle Casing. Fold Handle Casing over one handle and sew sts on Row 6 to sts on Rnd 19 of Body.

Repeat for remaining handle.

LINING

Using Bag as a guide and adding ½" (12 mm) seam allowances, cut fabric needed for inside of Bag excluding Handle Casings and last 2 rnds of Body. With **right** side of fabric together, sew side seams of Bag lining. Turn raw edges of lining to wrong side, then hand sew lining to inside of Bag along seams of Handle Casings and across the top of Rnd 19.

Messenger Bag

INTERMEDIATE

Finished Size: 11" (28 cm) square
(excluding Flap and Strap)

SHOPPING LIST

Yarn (Medium Weight Cotton) MEDIUM 4

[4 ounces, 200 yards
(113 grams, 184 meters) per skein**]**:

- ☐ 4 skeins

Crochet Hooks

- ☐ Size H (5 mm) **and**
- ☐ Size I (5.5 mm)
  or sizes needed for gauge

Additional Supplies

- ☐ ½ yard (.5 meter) Fabric for lining (optional)
  Note: Lining the Strap is recommended.
- ☐ Sewing needle
- ☐ Matching thread

GAUGE INFORMATION

With larger size hook,
in Body pattern,
16 sts and Rnds 1-7 = 4" (10 cm)

Gauge Swatch:
2¼" wide x 4" high
(5.75 cm x 10 cm)

Work same as Strap through Row 6.

STITCH GUIDE

FRONT POST DOUBLE CROCHET
(abbreviated FPdc)

YO, insert hook from **front** to **back** around post of st indicated *(Fig. 3, page 46)*, YO and pull up a loop (3 loops on hook), (YO and draw through 2 loops on hook) twice.

BACK POST DOUBLE CROCHET
(abbreviated BPdc)

YO, insert hook from **back** to **front** around post of st indicated *(Fig. 3, page 46)*, YO and pull up a loop (3 loops on hook), (YO and draw through 2 loops on hook) twice.

FRONT POST TREBLE CROCHET
(abbreviated FPtr)

YO twice, insert hook from **front** to **back** around post of st indicated *(Fig. 3, page 46)*, YO and pull up a loop (4 loops on hook), (YO and draw through 2 loops on hook) 3 times.

BACK POST TREBLE CROCHET
(abbreviated BPtr)

YO twice, insert hook from **back** to **front** around post of st indicated *(Fig. 3, page 46)*, YO and pull up a loop (4 loops on hook), (YO and draw through 2 loops on hook) 3 times.

INSTRUCTIONS

Strap

With larger hook, ch 12.

Row 1 (Wrong side)**:** Dc in fourth ch from hook **(3 skipped chs count as first dc)** and in each ch across: 10 dc.

Note: Loop a short piece of yarn around **back** of any stitch on Row 1 to mark **right** side.

Row 2: Ch 3 (**counts as first dc, now and throughout**), turn; ★ skip next 2 sts, work FPtr around next 2 sts, working in **front** of FPtr just made, work FPtr around 2 skipped sts; repeat from ★ once **more**, dc in last dc.

Row 3: Ch 3, turn; work BPtr around next 2 FPtr, skip next 2 FPtr, work BPtr around next 2 FPtr, working **behind** BPtr just made, work BPtr around 2 skipped FPtr, work BPtr around next 2 FPtr, dc in last dc.

Repeat Rows 2 and 3, 27 times **or** until desired length; then repeat Row 2 once **more**.

Last Row: Ch 3, turn; work BPdc around next 8 FPtr, dc in last dc; finish off.

Bottom

With larger size hook, ch 37; place marker in second ch from hook for st placement.

Row 1: Hdc in second ch from hook and in each ch across: 36 hdc.

Rows 2-4: Ch 1, turn; hdc in each hdc across; at end of Row 4, do **not** finish off.

Body

Rnd 1: Ch 2 (**does not count as a st, now and throughout**), turn; dc in first hdc and in each hdc across to last hdc, 2 dc in last hdc; skip first row, 2 dc in end of next 3 rows; working in free loops of beginning ch *(Fig. 2b, page 46)*, 2 dc in first ch, dc in next ch and in each ch across to marked ch, 2 dc in marked ch, remove marker; 2 dc in end of first 3 rows, skip last row, dc in same st as first dc; join with slip st to first dc: 88 dc.

Rnd 2 (Right side)**:** Ch 2, turn; † skip next 2 sts, work FPtr around next 2 sts, working in **front** of FPtr just made, work FPtr around 2 skipped sts †; repeat from † to † once **more**, ♥ skip next 2 sts, work FPtr around next 2 sts, working **behind** FPtr just made, work FPtr around 2 skipped sts ♥, repeat from † to † 6 times, repeat from ♥ to ♥ once, repeat from † to † 3 times, repeat from ♥ to ♥ once, repeat from † to † 6 times, repeat from ♥ to ♥ once, repeat from † to † once; join with slip st to first FPtr.

Rnd 3: Ch 2, turn; ★ work BPdc around next 8 FPtr, work BPtr around next 2 FPtr, † skip next 2 FPtr, work BPtr around next 2 FPtr, working **behind** BPtr just made, work BPtr around 2 skipped FPtr †; repeat from † to † 3 times **more**, work BPtr around next 2 FPtr, work BPdc around next 8 FPtr, work BPtr around next 2 FPtr, repeat from † to † once, work BPtr around next 2 FPtr; repeat from ★ once **more**; join with slip st to first BPtr.

Rnds 4-16: Repeat Rnds 2 and 3, 6 times; then repeat Rnd 2 once **more**.

Rnd 17: Ch 2, turn; work BPdc around next 8 sts, work BPtr around next 2 FPtr, ★ skip next 2 FPtr, work BPtr around next 2 FPtr, working **behind** BPtr just made, work BPtr around 2 skipped FPtr; repeat from ★ 3 times **more**, work BPtr around next 2 FPtr, work BPdc around next 8 FPtr, place marker around last BPdc made for st placement, work BPdc around last 52 sts; join with slip st to first BPdc, finish off.

Bag Flap

Row 1: With **right** side facing, join yarn with slip st in marked st; ch 3, skip next 2 sts, work FPtr around next 2 sts, working **behind** FPtr just made, work FPtr around 2 skipped sts, † skip next 2 sts, work FPtr around next 2 sts, working in **front** of FPtr just made, work FPtr around 2 skipped sts †; repeat from † to † 5 times **more**, skip next 2 sts, work FPtr around next 2 sts, working **behind** FPtr just made, work FPtr around 2 skipped sts, repeat from † to † once, dc in turning ch-2 on Rnd 17: 38 sts.

Row 2: Ch 3, turn; work BPdc around next 8 FPtr, work BPtr around next 2 FPtr, † skip next 2 FPtr, work BPtr around next 2 FPtr, working **behind** BPtr just made, work BPtr around 2 skipped FPtr †; repeat from † to † 3 times **more**, work BPtr around next 2 FPtr, work BPdc around next 8 FPtr, dc in last dc.

Row 3: Ch 3, turn; skip next 2 sts, work FPtr around next 2 sts, working **behind** FPtr just made, work FPtr around 2 skipped sts, † skip next 2 sts, work FPtr around next 2 sts, working in **front** of FPtr just made, work FPtr around 2 skipped sts †; repeat from † to † 5 times **more**, skip next 2 sts, work FPtr around next 2 sts, working **behind** FPtr just made, work FPtr around 2 skipped sts, repeat from † to † once, dc in last dc.

Rows 4-18: Repeat Rows 2 and 3, 7 times; then repeat Row 2 once **more**.

Change to smaller size hook.

Rnd 1: Ch 1, turn; sc in each st across to last dc, (sc, ch 2, sc) in last dc; working in ends of rows, sc evenly across, sc in each unworked st across Rnd 17; working in ends of rows, sc evenly across, sc in same st as first sc; ch 2; join with slip st to first sc.

Rnd 2: Ch 1, working from **left** to **right**, work reverse sc *(Figs. 4a-d, page 47)* in each sc and each corner ch-2 sp around; join with slip st to first st, finish off.

Finishing

OPTIONAL LINING

Using Bag as a guide and adding ½" (12 mm) seam allowances, cut fabric needed for inside of Bag including Flap. With **right** side of fabric together, sew side seams of Bag lining. Turn raw edges of lining to wrong side, then hand sew lining to inside of Bag and Flap.

Using the Strap as a guide, cut fabric for lining twice the width of the Strap and 1" (2.5 cm) longer.

With **right** side of fabric together, sew across length of lining. Turn lining right side out and place seam at center of one side. Turn raw edges at each end ½" (12 mm) to the inside of the lining and press.

With **wrong** side of Strap and seam side of lining together, hand sew lining to Strap.

Hand sew Strap ends securely to inside of Bag.

Braided Tablet Cover

INTERMEDIATE

Finished Size: 8" wide x 9½" deep (20.5 cm x 24 cm)

SHOPPING LIST

Yarn (Medium Weight) MEDIUM 4

[7 ounces, 370 yards

(198 grams, 338 meters) per skein**]**:

- ☐ 1 skein

Crochet Hook

- ☐ Size H (5 mm)

  or size needed for gauge

Additional Supplies

- ☐ 1" (25 mm) Button
- ☐ Sewing needle
- ☐ Matching thread
- ☐ Sewing pins

GAUGE INFORMATION

In Body pattern,
12 sts (2 repeats) and
6 rows = 3" (7.5 cm)

Gauge Swatch: 4" (10 cm)

Ch 18.

Row 1: Dc in third ch from hook and in each ch across: 16 dc.

Rows 2-6: Work same as Body.

Finish off.

STITCH GUIDE

FRONT POST DOUBLE CROCHET *(abbreviated FPdc)*

YO, insert hook from **front** to **back** around post of st indicated *(Fig. 3, page 46)*, YO and pull up a loop (3 loops on hook), (YO and draw through 2 loops on hook) twice.

BACK POST DOUBLE CROCHET *(abbreviated BPdc)*

YO, insert hook from **back** to **front** around post of st indicated *(Fig. 3, page 46)*, YO and pull up a loop (3 loops on hook), (YO and draw through 2 loops on hook) twice.

FRONT POST TREBLE CROCHET *(abbreviated FPtr)*

YO twice, insert hook from **front** to **back** around post of st indicated *(Fig. 3, page 46)*, YO and pull up a loop (4 loops on hook), (YO and draw through 2 loops on hook) 3 times.

BACK POST TREBLE CROCHET *(abbreviated BPtr)*

YO twice, insert hook from **back** to **front** around post of st indicated *(Fig. 3, page 46)*, YO and pull up a loop (4 loops on hook), (YO and draw through 2 loops on hook) 3 times.

INSTRUCTIONS

Body

Ch 30.

Row 1: Dc in third ch from hook and in each ch across: 28 dc.

Row 2 (Right side)**:** Ch 3 **(counts as first dc, now and throughout)**, turn; dc in next st, ★ skip next 2 sts, work FPtr around next 2 sts, working in **front** of FPtr just made, work FPtr around 2 skipped sts, work FPtr around next 2 sts; repeat from ★ across to last 2 sts, dc in last 2 sts.

Note: Loop a short piece of yarn around any stitch to mark Row 2 as **right** side.

Row 3: Ch 3, turn; dc in next dc, ★ skip next 2 FPtr, work BPtr around next 2 FPtr, working **behind** BPtr just made, work BPtr around 2 skipped FPtr, work BPtr around next 2 FPtr; repeat from ★ across to last 2 dc, dc in last 2 dc.

Rows 4-41: Repeat Rows 2 and 3, 19 times.

Row 42: Ch 3, turn; dc in next dc, work FPdc around each st across to last 2 dc, dc in last 2 dc.

Row 43: Ch 3, turn; dc in next dc, work BPdc around each FPdc across, dc in last 2 dc.

Row 44: Ch 1, turn; sc in first 2 sts, ch 3, skip next 3 BPdc (buttonhole), sc in next BPdc and in each st across: 25 sc and one ch-3 sp.

Row 45: Ch 1, turn; sc in each sc across to next ch-3 sp, 3 sc in ch-3 sp, sc in each sc across: 28 sc.

Row 46: Ch 1, turn; sc in each sc across; finish off.

Fold Body with **wrong** side together and folded edge approximately 9½" (24 cm) from beginning ch. Pin sides of Body together. Turn Body so that **right** side of Row 46 is facing.

Side Joining Row: Working in ends of rows through **both** layers, join yarn with sc ***(see Joining With Sc, page 45)*** at side edge of bottom fold; sc evenly across to Row 46; 3 sc in first sc, sc in each sc across to last sc, 3 sc in last sc; sc evenly across ends of rows to bottom fold, working through **both** layers; do **not** finish off.

Next Row: Ch 1, do **not** turn; working from **left** to **right**, work reverse sc ***(Figs. 4a-d, page 47)*** in each sc across; finish off.

Sew button to Body opposite buttonhole.

Braided Columns Tablet Cover

INTERMEDIATE

Finished Size: 9¼" wide x 11½" deep (23.5 cm x 29 cm)

SHOPPING LIST

Yarn (Medium Weight Cotton)

MEDIUM 4

[12 ounces, 608 yards
(340 grams, 556 meters) per skein**]**:

- ☐ 1 skein

Crochet Hook

- ☐ Size H (5 mm)
  or size needed for gauge

Additional Supplies

- ☐ 1" (25 mm) Buttons - 3
- ☐ Sewing needle
- ☐ Matching thread
- ☐ Sewing pins

GAUGE INFORMATION

In Body pattern,
one repeat (10 sts) = 2¾" (7 cm);
8 rows = 4" (10 cm)

Gauge Swatch: 4" (10 cm) square
Ch 17.

Row 1: Hdc in third ch from hook and in each ch across: 15 hdc.

Rows 2-8: Ch 2 (**counts as first hdc**), turn; hdc in next st and in each st across.
Finish off.

STITCH GUIDE

BACK POST DOUBLE CROCHET *(abbreviated BPdc)*

YO, insert hook from **back** to **front** around post of st indicated *(Fig. 3, page 46)*, YO and pull up a loop (3 loops on hook), (YO and draw through 2 loops on hook) twice.

FRONT POST TREBLE CROCHET *(abbreviated FPtr)*

YO twice, insert hook from **front** to **back** around post of st indicated *(Fig. 3, page 46)*, YO and pull up a loop (4 loops on hook), (YO and draw through 2 loops on hook) 3 times.

BACK POST TREBLE CROCHET *(abbreviated BPtr)*

YO twice, insert hook from **back** to **front** around post of st indicated *(Fig. 3, page 46)*, YO and pull up a loop (4 loops on hook), (YO and draw through 2 loops on hook) 3 times.

INSTRUCTIONS

Body

Ch 34.

Row 1 (Wrong side)**:** Dc in fourth ch from hook (**3 skipped chs count as first dc**) and in each ch across: 32 dc.

Note: Loop a short piece of yarn around **back** of any stitch on Row 1 to mark **right** side.

Row 2: Ch 2 (**does not count as a st, now and throughout**), turn; hdc in first 3 sts, ★ † skip next 2 sts, work FPtr around next 2 sts, working in **front** of FPtr just made, work FPtr around 2 skipped sts, work FPtr around next 2 sts †, hdc in next 4 sts; repeat from ★ once **more**, then repeat from † to † once, hdc in last 3 sts.

Row 3: Ch 2, turn; hdc in first 3 hdc, ★ † skip next 2 FPtr, work BPtr around next 2 FPtr, working **behind** BPtr just made, work BPtr around 2 skipped FPtr, work BPtr around next 2 FPtr †, hdc in next 4 hdc; repeat from ★ once **more**, then repeat from † to † once, hdc in last 3 hdc.

Repeat Rows 2 and 3 for pattern until Body measures approximately 26½" (67.5 cm) from beginning ch, ending by working Row 2.

Band

Row 1: Ch 2, turn; hdc in first 3 hdc, work BPdc around next 6 FPtr, (hdc in next 4 hdc, work BPdc around next 6 FPtr) twice, hdc in last 3 hdc.

Row 2: Ch 1, turn; sc in each st across.

Row 3: Ch 1, turn; sc in first 5 sc, ch 2, skip next 2 sc (buttonhole), ★ sc in next 8 sc, ch 2, skip next 2 sc; repeat from ★ once **more**, sc in last 5 sc: 26 sc and 3 ch-2 sps.

Row 4: Ch 1, turn; sc in first 5 sc, 2 sc in next ch-2 sp, ★ sc in next 8 sc, 2 sc in next ch-2 sp; repeat from ★ once **more**, sc in last 5 sc: 32 sc.

Row 5: Ch 1, turn; sc in each sc across; finish off.

Fold Body with **wrong** side together and folded edge approximately 11½" (29 cm) from beginning ch; pin sides together. Turn Body so that **right** side of Row 5 of Band is facing.

Side Joining Row: Working in ends of rows through **both** layers, join yarn with sc *(see Joining With Sc, page 45)* at side edge of bottom fold; sc evenly across to Row 5 of Band; 3 sc in first sc, sc in each sc across to last sc, 3 sc in last sc; sc evenly across ends of rows to opposite side edge of bottom fold, working through **both** layers; do **not** finish off.

Next Row: Ch 1, do **not** turn; working from **left** to **right**, work reverse sc *(Figs. 4a-d, page 47)* in each sc across; finish off.

Sew 3 buttons to Body opposite buttonholes.

Diamonds & Cables Backpack

INTERMEDIATE

Finished Size: 15¼" wide x 19" deep (38.5 cm x 48.5 cm)

SHOPPING LIST

Yarn (Medium Weight Cotton) MEDIUM 4

[4 ounces, 200 yards
(113 grams, 184 meters) per skein]:

☐ 4 skeins

Crochet Hooks

☐ Size H (5 mm),

☐ Size I (5.5 mm), **and**

☐ Size J (6 mm)
or sizes needed for gauge

☐ Size L (8 mm) (for straps only)

Additional Supplies

Parachute 550 Cord
[100 feet (30.5 meters) per package]:

☐ White - 1 package (for straps only)

☐ Beads -18 (optional)

GAUGE INFORMATION

With medium size hook,
12 sc and 13 rows = 4" (10 cm)

Gauge Swatch: 4" (10 cm) square

With medium size hook, ch 13.

Row 1: Sc in second ch from hook and in each ch across: 12 sc.

Rows 2-13: Ch 1, turn; sc in each sc across.

Finish off.

STITCH GUIDE

FRONT POST TREBLE CROCHET
(abbreviated FPtr)

YO twice, insert hook from **front** to **back** around post of sc indicated *(Fig. 3, page 46)*, YO and pull up a loop (4 loops on hook), (YO and draw through 2 loops on hook) 3 times.

CABLE

Ch 3, skip next 2 sc, sc in next sc, **turn**; sc in next 3 chs, slip st in first sc made **(Cable made)**, **turn**; working **behind** Cable, sc in 2 skipped sc *(Figs. A-E)*.

Fig. A

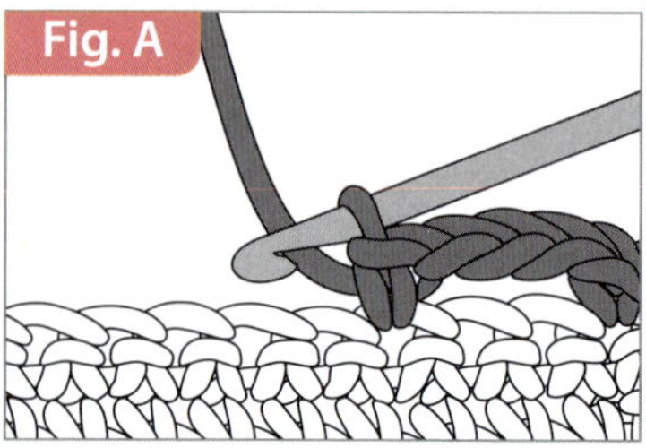

Fig. B

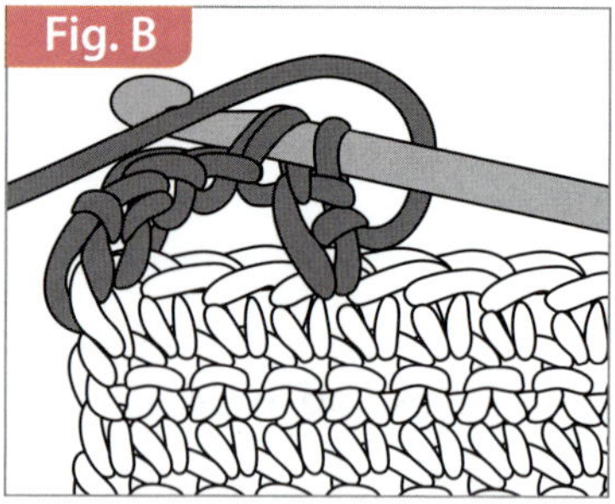

Fig. C

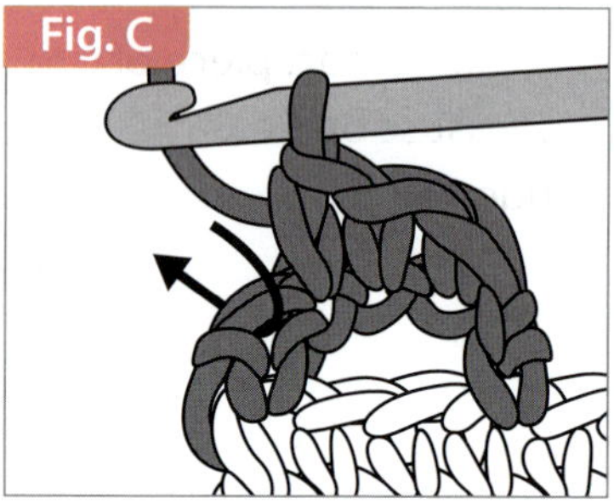

Fig. D

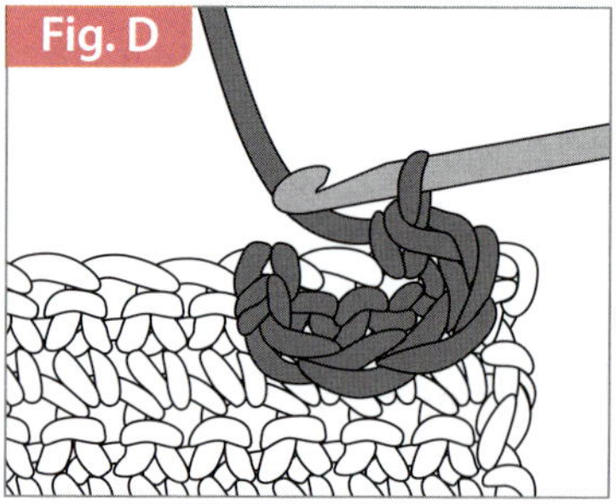

Fig. E

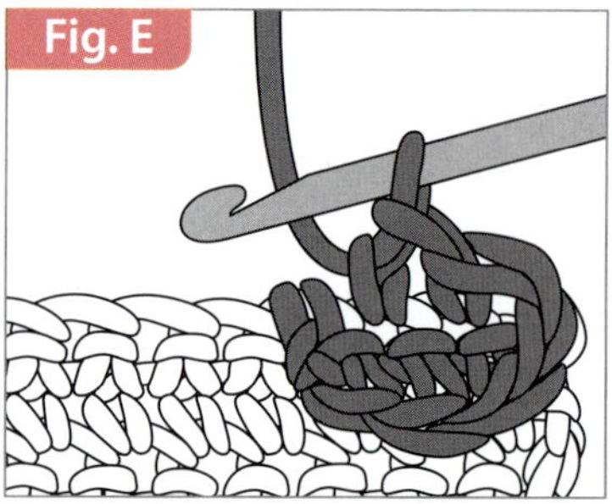

INSTRUCTIONS

Panel (Make 2)

With larger size hook, ch 51.

Row 1 (Wrong side)**:** Sc in second ch from hook and in each ch across: 50 sc.

Note: Loop a short piece of yarn around last sc on Row 1 to mark top edge.

Row 2: Ch 1, turn; working in Front Loops Only *(Fig. 1, page 46)*, slip st in each st across.

Row 3: Ch 1, turn; working in free loops of previous row *(Fig. 2a, page 46)*, sc in each st across.

Row 4: Ch 1, turn; sc in first sc, work Cables across to last sc, sc in last sc: 16 Cables and 34 sc.

Row 5: Ch 1, turn; sc in first sc, working in **front** of Cables, 2 sc in next sc, (sc in next sc, 2 sc in next sc) across to last 2 sc, sc in last 2 sc: 50 sc.

Row 6: Ch 1, turn; slip st in Front Loop Only of each sc across.

Row 7: Ch 1, turn; working in free loops of previous row, sc in each st across to last 3 sts, place marker around last sc made for st placement, sc in last 3 sts.

Change to medium size hook.

Rows 8 and 9: Ch 1, turn; sc in each sc across.

Row 10: Ch 1, turn; sc in first sc, work FPtr around marked sc, remove marker, skip sc behind FPtr, sc in next 4 sc, work FPtr around next sc from last FPtr made, ★ skip next 4 sc from last FPtr made, work FPtr around next sc, skip 2 sc behind 2 FPtr, sc in next 4 sc, work FPtr around next sc from last FPtr made; repeat from ★ across to last 2 sc, skip sc behind FPtr, sc in last sc.

Row 11: Ch 1, turn; sc in each st across to last 2 sts, place marker around last sc made for st placement, sc in last 2 sts.

Rows 12 and 13: Ch 1, turn; sc in each sc across.

Row 14: Ch 1, turn; sc in first 3 sc, work FPtr around marked sc, remove marker, skip next 4 sc from last FPtr made, work FPtr around next sc, ★ skip 2 sc behind FPtr, sc in next 4 sc, work FPtr around next sc from last FPtr made, skip next 4 sc from last FPtr made, work FPtr around next sc; repeat from ★ across to last 5 sc, skip 2 sc behind FPtr, sc in last 3 sc.

Row 15: Ch 1, turn; sc in each st across to last 3 sc, place marker around last sc made for st placement, sc in last 3 sc.

Rows 16 and 17: Ch 1, turn; sc in each sc across.

Rows 18-46: Repeat Rows 10-17, 3 times; then repeat Rows 10-14 once **more**.

Row 47: Ch 1, turn; sc in each st across.

Change to larger size hook.

Rows 48-53: Repeat Rows 2-7.

Row 54: Ch 1, turn; sc in each sc across.

Change to smallest size hook.

Trim: Ch 1, do **not** turn; work 50 sc evenly spaced across ends of rows, ch 2; working in free loops of beginning ch *(Fig. 2b, page 46)*, sc in each ch across, ch 2; work 50 sc evenly spaced across ends of rows; ch 2, sc in each sc across Row 54, ch 2; join with slip st to first sc, finish off: 200 sc and 4 ch-2 sps.

SIDES AND BOTTOM JOINING

With **wrong** sides and top edges together, join yarn with slip st in upper corner ch-2 sp; ch 1, working from **left** to **right** through **both** loops of each sc on **both** pieces, work reverse sc *(Figs. 4a-d, page 47)* across 3 sides, working one reverse sc in each ch-2 sp, ending in next upper ch-2 sp; slip st in same sp as last reverse sc; do **not** finish off.

TOP BORDER

Rnd 1 (Eyelet rnd)**:** Ch 3 **(counts as first dc, now and throughout)**, do **not** turn; working in sts and sps around top opening, † skip next joining, dc in next sp, ch 2, skip next sc, 2 dc in next sc, ch 2, skip next 2 sc, (dc in next 2 sc, ch 2, skip next 2 sc) 11 times, 2 dc in next sc, ch 2, skip next sc †, dc in next sp, repeat from † to † once; join with slip st to first dc: 56 dc and 28 ch-2 sps.

Rnd 2: Ch 3, dc in next dc, 2 dc in next ch-2 sp, (dc in next 2 dc, 2 dc in next ch-2 sp) around; join with slip st to first dc: 112 dc.

Rnd 3: Ch 1, (sc, ch 3, sc) in same st as joining, skip next dc, ★ (sc, ch 3, dc) in next dc, skip next dc; repeat from ★ around; join with slip st to first sc, finish off.

Finishing

STRAP (Make 2)

With largest size hook, parachute cord, and leaving a 12" (30.5 cm) length for knotting at each end, crochet a chain 66" (167.5 cm) long, making sure that both Straps are the same length.

Beginning at one side edge, weave one Strap through Eyelet Rnd, ending at same side edge.

Beginning at opposite side edge, weave remaining Strap through Eyelet Rnd in same manner.

Hold together both long ends of one Strap and make an overhand knot as close as possible to last chains. With smallest size hook, pull long ends of Strap through space on bottom corner at same side edge. Tie an overhand knot with long ends as close as possible to corner.

Thread beads as desired onto each long end and make an overhand knot at each end. Trim ends.

Repeat with opposite Strap.

Ribbed & Cabled Phone Cozy

EASY +

Finished Size: 5¼" wide x 8¼" deep (13.25 cm x 21 cm)

SHOPPING LIST

Yarn (Medium Weight) MEDIUM 4

[3.5 ounces, 270 yards
(100 grams, 247 meters) per skein]:

- ☐ 1 skein

Crochet Hook

- ☐ Size H (5 mm)
  or size needed for gauge

SAMSUNG

GAUGE INFORMATION

In Body pattern,

18 sts and 12 rnds = 4" (10 cm)

Gauge Swatch:

5¼" wide x 4" high

(13.25 cm x 10 cm)

Work same as Body through Rnd 12.

STITCH GUIDE

BACK POST DOUBLE CROCHET

(abbreviated BPdc)

YO, insert hook from **back** to **front** around post of st indicated ***(Fig. 3, page 46)***, YO and pull up a loop (3 loops on hook), (YO and draw through 2 loops on hook) twice.

FRONT POST DOUBLE CROCHET

(abbreviated FPdc)

YO, insert hook from **front** to **back** around post of st indicated ***(Fig. 3, page 46)***, YO and pull up a loop (3 loops on hook), (YO and draw through 2 loops on hook) twice.

FRONT POST TREBLE CROCHET

(abbreviated FPtr)

YO twice, insert hook from **front** to **back** around post of st indicated ***(Fig. 3, page 46)***, YO and pull up a loop (4 loops on hook), (YO and draw through 2 loops on hook) 3 times.

INSTRUCTIONS

Body

Ch 24.

Rnd 1 (Wrong side)**:** Dc in third ch from hook **(2 skipped chs do not count as a st)** and in each ch across to last ch, 4 dc in last ch; working in free loops of beginning ch ***(Fig. 2b, page 46)***, dc in each ch across to same ch as first dc, 3 dc in same ch; join with slip st to first dc: 48 dc.

Rnd 2: Ch 2 **(does not count as a st, now and throughout)**, turn; (work FPdc around next st, work BPdc around next st) 4 times, † skip next 2 sts, work FPtr around next 2 sts, working **behind** FPtr just made, work FPtr around 2 skipped sts, skip next 2 sts, work FPtr around next 2 sts, working in **front** of FPtr just made, work FPtr around 2 skipped sts, work BPdc around next st †, (work FPdc around next st, work BPdc around next st) 8 times, repeat from † to † once, (work FPdc around next st, work BPdc around next st) 3 times; join with slip st to first FPdc.

Rnd 3: Ch 2, turn; work FPdc around next st, (work BPdc around next st, work FPdc around next st) 3 times, work BPdc around next 8 FPtr, work FPdc around next st, (work BPdc around next st, work FPdc around next st) 8 times, work BPdc around next 8 FPtr, (work FPdc around next st, work BPdc around next st) 4 times; join with slip st to first FPdc.

Rnds 4-20: Repeat Rnds 2 and 3, 8 times; then repeat Rnd 2 once **more**.

Rnd 21: Ch 2, turn; (work FPdc around next st, work BPdc around next st) 4 times, † work FPdc around next 2 sts, skip next st, work FPdc around next 5 sts, work BPdc around next st †, (work FPdc around next st, work BPdc around next st) 8 times, repeat from † to † once, (work FPdc around next st, work BPdc around next st) 3 times; join with slip st to first FPdc: 46 sts.

Rnds 22-25: Ch 2, turn; (work FPdc around next st, work BPdc around next st) around; join with slip st to first FPdc.

Finish off.

Petite Shoulder Bag

INTERMEDIATE

Finished Size: 6" wide x 8½" deep (15.25 cm x 21.5 cm)

SHOPPING LIST

Yarn (Medium Weight) MEDIUM 4

[2.5 ounces, 153 yards

(70 grams, 140 meters) per skein**]**:

- ☐ 1 skein

Crochet Hook

- ☐ Size J (6 mm)
  or size needed for gauge

Additional Supplies

- ☐ Yarn needle
- ☐ 1" (25 mm) Button
- ☐ Sewing needle
- ☐ Matching thread
- ☐ Sewing pins

GAUGE INFORMATION

In Body pattern,

2 repeats and 8 rows = 4" (10 cm)

Gauge Swatch: 6" wide x 4" high (15.25 cm x 10 cm)

Work same as Body through Row 8: 20 sts and 3 ch-2 sps.

STITCH GUIDE

FRONT POST TREBLE CROCHET *(abbreviated FPtr)*

YO twice, insert hook from **front** to **back** around post of st indicated *(Fig. 3, page 46)*, YO and pull up a loop (4 loops on hook), (YO and draw through 2 loops on hook) 3 times.

BACK POST TREBLE CROCHET *(abbreviated BPtr)*

YO twice, insert hook from **back** to **front** around post of st indicated *(Fig. 3, page 46)*, YO and pull up a loop (4 loops on hook), (YO and draw through 2 loops on hook) 3 times.

INSTRUCTIONS

Body

Ch 26.

Row 1: Sc in second ch from hook, skip next 2 chs, dc in next ch, (dc, ch 2, dc) in next ch, dc in next ch, ★ skip next 2 chs, sc in next ch, skip next 2 chs, dc in next ch, (dc, ch 2, dc) in next ch, dc in next ch; repeat from ★ once **more**, skip next 2 chs, sc in last ch: 16 sts and 3 ch-2 sps.

Row 2 (Right side)**:** Ch 3 **(counts as first dc, now and throughout)**, turn; work FPtr around next dc, (2 dc, ch 2, 2 dc) in next ch-2 sp, skip next dc, work FPtr around next dc, ★ skip next sc, work FPtr around next dc, (2 dc, ch 2, 2 dc) in next ch-2 sp, skip next dc, work FPtr around next dc; repeat from ★ once **more**, dc in last sc: 20 sts and 3 ch-2 sps.

Note: Loop a short piece of yarn around any stitch to mark Row 2 as **right** side.

Row 3: Ch 3, turn; work BPtr around next FPtr, (3 dc, ch 1, 3 dc) in next ch-2 sp, skip next 2 dc, work BPtr around next FPtr, ★ ch 1, work BPtr around next FPtr, (3 dc, ch 1, 3 dc) in next ch-2 sp, skip next 2 dc, work BPtr around next FPtr; repeat from ★ once **more**, dc in last dc: 26 sts and 5 ch-1 sps.

Row 4: Ch 3, turn; dc in same st, work FPtr around next BPtr, sc in next ch-1 sp, skip next 3 dc, work FPtr around next BPtr, ★ (dc, ch 2, dc) in next ch-1 sp, work FPtr around next BPtr, sc in next ch-1 sp, skip next 3 dc, work FPtr around next BPtr; repeat from ★ once **more**, 2 dc in last dc: 17 sts and 2 ch-2 sps.

Row 5: Ch 3, turn; 2 dc in same st, skip next dc, work BPtr around next FPtr, skip next sc, work BPtr around next FPtr, ★ (2 dc, ch 2, 2 dc) in next ch-2 sp, skip next dc, work BPtr around next FPtr, skip next sc, work BPtr around next FPtr; repeat from ★ once **more**, skip next dc, 3 dc in last dc: 20 sts and 2 ch-2 sps.

Row 6: Ch 3, turn; 3 dc in same st, skip next 2 dc, work FPtr around next BPtr, ch 1, work FPtr around next BPtr, ★ (3 dc, ch 1, 3 dc) in next ch-2 sp, skip next 2 dc, work FPtr around next BPtr, ch 1, work FPtr around next BPtr; repeat from ★ once **more**, skip next 2 dc, 4 dc in last dc: 26 sts and 5 ch-1 sps.

Row 7: Ch 1, turn; sc in first dc, skip next 3 dc, work BPtr around next FPtr, (dc, ch 2, dc) in next ch-1 sp, work BPtr around next FPtr, ★ sc in next ch-1 sp, skip next 3 dc, work BPtr around next FPtr, (dc, ch 2, dc) in next ch-1 sp, work BPtr around next FPtr; repeat from ★ once **more**, skip next 3 dc, sc in last dc: 16 sts and 3 ch-2 sps.

Row 8: Ch 3, turn; work FPtr around next BPtr, (2 dc, ch 2, 2 dc) in next ch-2 sp, skip next dc, work FPtr around next BPtr, ★ skip next sc, work FPtr around next BPtr, (2 dc, ch 2, 2 dc) in next ch-2 sp, skip next dc, work FPtr around next BPtr; repeat from ★ once **more**, dc in last sc: 20 sts and 3 ch-2 sps.

Rows 9-46: Repeat Rows 3-8, 6 times; then repeat Rows 3 and 4 once **more**: 17 sts and 2 ch-2 sps.

Finish off.

Finishing

Strap: Leaving a long end for sewing, ch 106, slip st in second ch from hook and in each ch across; finish off leaving a long end for sewing.

With **right** side together, fold piece, placing fold approximately 8" (20.5 cm) from last row.

Pin each side edge together, then sew side seams.

Thread yarn needle with one long end from Strap. Beginning approximately 2" (5 cm) from top edge of one side seam, sew Strap end to seam.

Sew opposite end of Strap to remaining side seam, beginning approximately 2" (5 cm) from top edge.

Turn Bag **right** side out and sew button to center, using center ch-2 sp on Row 2 as buttonhole.

Beaded Broomstick Lace Backpack

Shown on page 39.

INTERMEDIATE

Finished Size: 17¾" wide x 19" deep (45 cm x 48.5 cm)

SHOPPING LIST

Yarn (Medium Weight) MEDIUM 4

[14 ounces, 710 yards
(400 grams, 650 meters) per skein]:

- ☐ 1 skein

Crochet Hooks

- ☐ Size H (5 mm) **or** size needed for gauge
- ☐ Size B (2.25 mm)
  (or size that will go through hole of bead)
- ☐ Size M/N (9 mm) (for Straps only)

Knitting Needles

Straight,

- ☐ Size 50 (25 mm) - 3

Additional Supplies

Wooden Beads

- ☐ 10 mm for Body - 42
- ☐ Various sizes/shapes for strap decoration - 20

Hemp twine, 1/16" (1.5 mm)
[18 yards (16.5 meters) per ball]:

- ☐ 1 ball

GAUGE INFORMATION

14 sc and 12 rows = 4" (10 cm)
Rnds 1-6 = 3½" (9 cm)

Gauge Swatch: 4" wide x 3½" high (10 cm x 9 cm)

With medium size hook, ch 15.

Row 1: Sc in second ch from hook and in each ch across: 14 sc.

Rows 2-12: Ch 1, turn; sc in each sc across.

Finish off.

STITCH GUIDE

POPCORN

4 Sc in next sc or sp, drop loop from hook, insert hook in first sc of 4-sc group, hook dropped loop and draw through st, ch 1 to close.

BROOMSTICK LACE

Step A - Putting loops on knitting needle: Place loop from hook onto knitting needle *(Fig. A)*, ★ working from **left** to **right**, insert hook in next sc and pull up a loop, place loop on knitting needle; repeat from ★ across.

Fig. A

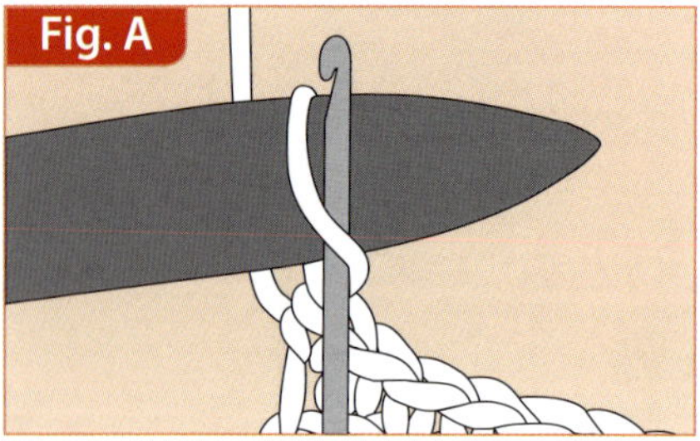

Step B - Working in loops: Insert hook in as many loops on knitting needle as instructed *(Fig. B)*, YO and draw through all loops on hook, ch 1 *(Fig. C)*, work as many sc as instructed in same loops *(Fig. D)*.

Fig. B

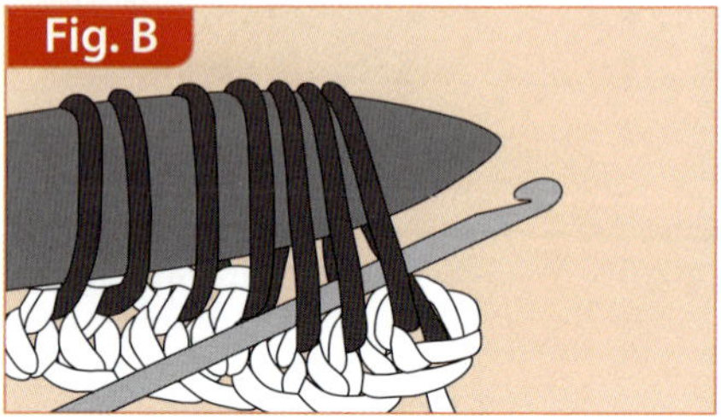

Fig. C

Fig. D

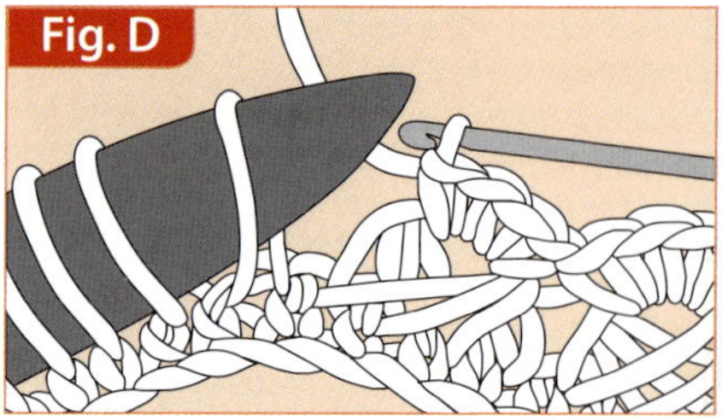

ADDING A BEAD

Slip loop from knitting needle, insert smallest size hook through bead, catch loop with hook ***(Fig. E)*** and slide bead onto loop ***(Fig. F)***.

Fig. E

Fig. F

INSTRUCTIONS

Body

With medium size hook, ch 61.

Rnd 1 (Right side)**:** Sc in second ch from hook and in each ch across to last ch, 4 sc in last ch; working in free loops of beginning ch ***(Fig. 2b, page 46)***, sc in each ch across to same ch as first sc, 3 sc in same ch; join with slip st to first sc: 124 sc.

Note: Loop a short piece of yarn around any stitch to mark Rnd 1 as **right** side.

Rnds 2 and 3: Ch 1, sc in same st as joining and in each sc around; join with slip st to first sc.

Rnd 4: Ch 1, sc in same st as joining, ch 1, skip next sc, work Popcorn in next sc, , skip next sc, ★ sc in next sc, ch 1, skip next sc, work Popcorn in next sc, skip next sc; repeat from ★ around; join with slip st to first sc: 31 sc, 31 Popcorns, and 31 ch-1 sps.

Rnd 5: Ch 1, **turn**; sc in next Popcorn **(ch at top of Popcorn, now and throughout)**, ch 1, sc in next ch-1 sp, ch 1, ★ skip next sc, sc in next Popcorn, ch 1, sc in next ch-1 sp, ch 1; repeat from ★ around; join with slip st to first sc: 62 sc and 62 ch-1 sps.

Rnd 6: Ch 1, turn; ★ work Popcorn in next ch-1 sp, skip next sc, sc in next ch-1 sp, ch 1; repeat from ★ around; join with slip st to first Popcorn: 31 sc, 31 Popcorns, and 31 ch-1 sps.

Rnd 7: Ch 1, turn; ★ sc in next ch-1 sp, ch 1, skip next sc, sc in next Popcorn, ch 1; repeat from ★ around; join with slip st to first sc: 62 sc and 62 ch-1 sps.

Rnd 8: Ch 1, turn; ★ sc in next ch-1 sp, ch 1, work Popcorn in next ch-1 sp; repeat from ★ around; join with slip st to first sc: 31 sc, 31 Popcorns, and 31 ch-1 sps.

Rnds 9-12: Repeat Rnds 5-8: 31 sc, 31 Popcorns, and 31 ch-1 sps.

Rnd 13: Ch 1, turn; 2 sc in each Popcorn and in each ch-1 sp around; join with slip st to first sc: 124 sc.

Rnd 14: Ch 1, turn; working in Front Loops Only ***(Fig. 1, page 46)***, slip st in next sc and in each sc around; join with slip st to **both** loops of first slip st.

Rnd 15: Ch 1, turn; working in free loops of sc on Rnd 13 ***(Fig. 2a, page 46)***, sc in each sc around; join with slip st to first sc.

Rnd 16 (Broomstick Lace - Step A)**:** With **right** side facing and working from **left** to **right**, place loop from hook onto knitting needle, ★ insert hook in next sc, YO and pull up a loop, place loop onto knitting needle; repeat from ★ around, placing 40 loops **each** on first and second needles and 44 loops on last needle ***(Photo A)***: 124 loops.

Photo A

Rnd 17 (Broomstick Lace - Step B)**:** With **right** side facing and working from **right** to **left**, insert hook in first 4 loops on last knitting needle, YO and pull up a loop, ch 1, 4 sc in same loops, leave loop on medium size hook when adding bead, using smallest size hook, add bead to next loop, with medium size hook, sc in bead loop, † insert hook in next 5 loops, work 5 sc in same loops, using smallest size hook, add bead to next loop, with medium size hook, sc in bead loop †; repeat from † to † 8 times **more**, insert hook in next 4 loops, work 4 sc in same loops, using smallest size hook, add bead to next loop, with medium size hook, sc in bead loop, repeat from † to † around; join with slip to to first sc: 124 sc.

Rnd 18: Ch 1, turn; sc in each sc around; join with slip st to first sc.

Rnd 19: Ch 1, turn; working in Front Loops Only, slip st in next sc and in each sc around; join with slip st to **both** loops of first slip st.

Rnd 20: Ch 1, turn; working in free loops of sc on previous rnd, sc in each sc around; join with slip st to first sc.

Rnd 21: Ch 1, turn; sc in same st as joining, ch 1, skip next sc, work Popcorn in next sc, ch 1, skip next sc, ★ sc in next sc, ch 1, skip next sc, work Popcorn in next sc, ch 1, skip next sc; repeat from ★ around; join with slip st to first sc: 31 sc, 31 Popcorns, and 31 ch-1 sps.

Rnds 22-33: Repeat Rnds 5-8, 3 times: 31 sc, 31 Popcorns, and 31 ch-1 sps.

Rnds 34-42: Repeat Rnds 13-21: 31 sc, 31 Popcorns, and 31 ch-1 sps.

Rnds 43-50: Repeat Rnds 5-8 twice: 31 sc, 31 Popcorns, and 31 ch-1 sps.

Rnd 51: Ch 1, turn; 2 sc in each Popcorn and each ch-1 sp around; join with slip st to first sc: 124 sc.

Rnd 52 (Eyelet rnd)**:** Ch 3 **(counts as first dc)**, turn; dc in next 6 sc, ch 5, (skip next 5 sc, dc in next 5 dc, ch 5) 4 times, (skip next 5 sc, dc in next 6 sc, ch 5) twice, skip next 5 sc, (dc in next 5 sc, ch 5, skip next 5 sc) around; join with slip st to first dc: 64 dc and 12 ch-5 sps.

Rnd 53: Ch 1, do **not** turn; sc in same st as joining and in each dc around working 5 sc in each ch-5 sp; join with slip st to first sc: 124 sc.

Rnds 54-56: Ch 1, sc in each sc around; join with slip st to first sc.

Finish off.

Finishing

STRAP (Make 2)

Using largest size crochet hook, hemp, and leaving a 12" (30.5 cm) length for knotting at each end, crochet a chain 66" (167.5 cm) long, making sure that both Straps are the same length.

Finish off.

Beginning at one side edge, weave one Strap through Eyelet Rnd, ending at same side edge.

Beginning at opposite side edge, weave remaining Strap through Eyelet Rnd in same manner.

Hold together both long ends of one Strap and make an overhand knot as close as possible to last chains. With medium size hook, pull long ends of Strap through bottom corner at same side edge. Tie an overhand knot with long ends as close as possible to corner.

Thread 5 beads as desired onto each long end and make an overhand knot at each end. Trim ends.

Repeat with opposite Strap.

GENERAL INSTRUCTIONS

ABBREVIATIONS

BPdc	Back Post double crochet(s)
BPtr	Back Post treble crochet(s)
ch(s)	chain(s)
cm	centimeters
dc	double crochet(s)
FPdc	Front Post double crochet(s)
FPtr	Front Post treble crochet(s)
hdc	half double crochet(s)
mm	millimeters
Rnd(s	Round(s)
sc	single crochet(s)
sp(s)	space(s)
st(s)	stitch(es)
YO	yarn over

CROCHET TERMINOLOGY		
UNITED STATES		INTERNATIONAL
slip stitch (slip st)	=	single crochet (sc)
single crochet (sc)	=	double crochet (dc)
half double crochet (hdc)	=	half treble crochet (htr)
double crochet (dc)	=	treble crochet (tr)
treble crochet (tr)	=	double treble crochet (dtr)
double treble crochet (dtr)	=	triple treble crochet (ttr)
triple treble crochet (tr tr)	=	quadruple treble crochet (qtr)
skip	=	miss

SYMBOLS & TERMS

★ — work instructions following ★ as many **more** times as indicated in addition to the first time.

† to † **or** ♥ to ♥ — work all instructions from first † or ♥ to second † or ♥ **as many** times as specified.

( ) or **[ ]** — work enclosed instructions as **many times** as specified by the number immediately following **or** work all enclosed instructions in the stitch or space indicated **or** contains explanatory remarks.

colon (:) — the number(s) given after a colon at the end of a row or round denote(s) the number of stitches or spaces you should have on that row or round.

BEGINNER	Projects for first-time crocheters using basic stitches. Minimal shaping.
EASY	Projects using yarn with basic stitches, repetitive stitch patterns, simple color changes, and simple shaping and finishing.
INTERMEDIATE	Projects using a variety of techniques, such as basic lace patterns or color patterns, mid-level shaping and finishing.
EXPERIENCED	Projects with intricate stitch patterns, techniques and dimension, such as non-repeating patterns, multi-color techniques, fine threads, small hooks, detailed shaping and refined finishing.

GAUGE

Exact gauge is **essential** for proper size. Before beginning your project, make the sample swatch given in the individual instructions in the yarn and hook specified. After completing the swatch, measure it, counting your stitches and rows/rounds carefully. If your swatch is larger or smaller than specified, **make another, changing hook size to get the correct gauge**. Keep trying until you find the size hook that will give you the specified gauge.

JOINING WITH SC

When instructed to join with sc, begin with a slip knot on hook. Insert hook in stitch or space indicated, YO and pull up a loop, YO and draw through both loops on hook.

CROCHET HOOKS	
U.S.	**Metric mm**
B-1	2.25
C-2	2.75
D-3	3.25
E-4	3.5
F-5	3.75
G-6	4
7	4.5
H-8	5
I-9	5.5
J-10	6
K-10½	6.5
L-11	8
M/N-13	9
N/P-15	10
P/Q	15
Q	16
S	19

Yarn Weight Symbol & Names	LACE 0	SUPER FINE 1	FINE 2	LIGHT 3	MEDIUM 4	BULKY 5	SUPER BULKY 6	JUMBO 7
Type of Yarns in Category	Fingering, size 10 crochet thread	Sock, Fingering, Baby	Sport, Baby	DK, Light Worsted	Worsted, Afghan, Aran	Chunky, Craft, Rug	Super Bulky, Roving	Jumbo, Roving
Crochet Gauge* Ranges in Single Crochet to 4" (10 cm)	32-42 sts**	21-32 sts	16-20 sts	12-17 sts	11-14 sts	8-11 sts	6-9 sts	5 sts and fewer
Advised Hook Size Range	Steel*** 6 to 8, Regular hook B-1	B-1 to E-4	E-4 to 7	7 to I-9	I-9 to K-10½	K-10½ to M/N-13	M/N-13 to Q	Q and larger

*GUIDELINES ONLY: The chart above reflects the most commonly used gauges and hook sizes for specific yarn categories.

** Lace weight yarns are usually crocheted with larger hooks to create lacy openwork patterns. Accordingly, a gauge range is difficult to determine. Always follow the gauge stated in your pattern.

*** Steel crochet hooks are sized differently from regular hooks–the higher the number, the smaller the hook, which is the reverse of regular hook sizing.

FRONT LOOP ONLY

Work only in loop(s) indicated by arrow *(Fig. 1)*.

Fig. 1

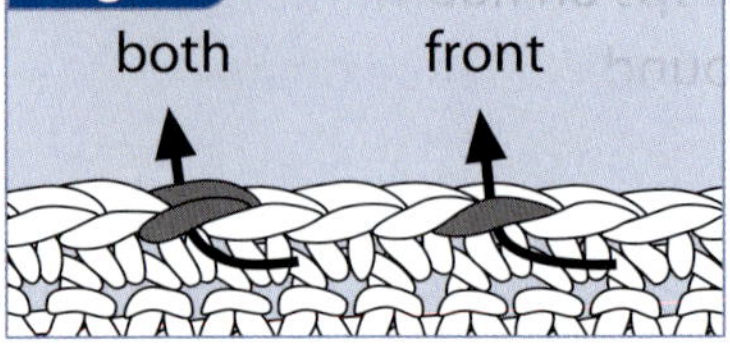

When instructed to work in free loops of a beginning ch, work in loop indicated by arrow *(Fig. 2b)*.

Fig. 2b

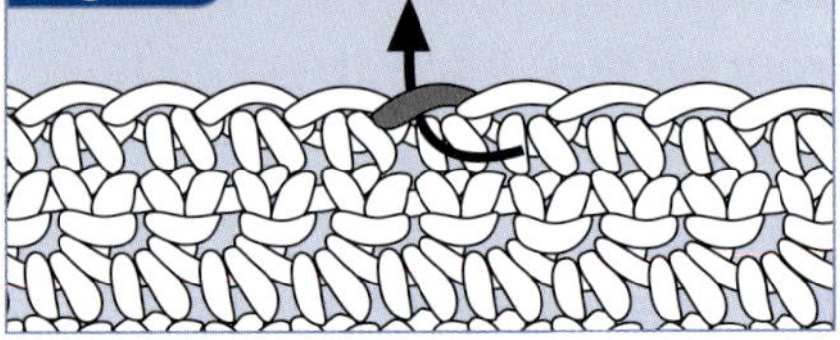

FREE LOOPS

After working in Back or Front Loops Only on a row or round, there will be a ridge of unused loops. These are called the free loops. Later, where instructed to work in the free loops of the same row or round, work in these loops *(Fig. 2a)*.

Fig. 2a

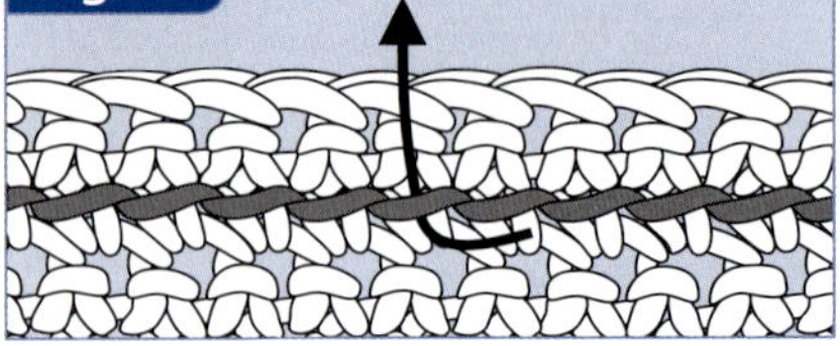

POST STITCH

Work around post of stitch indicated, inserting hook in direction of arrow *(Fig. 3)*.

Fig. 3

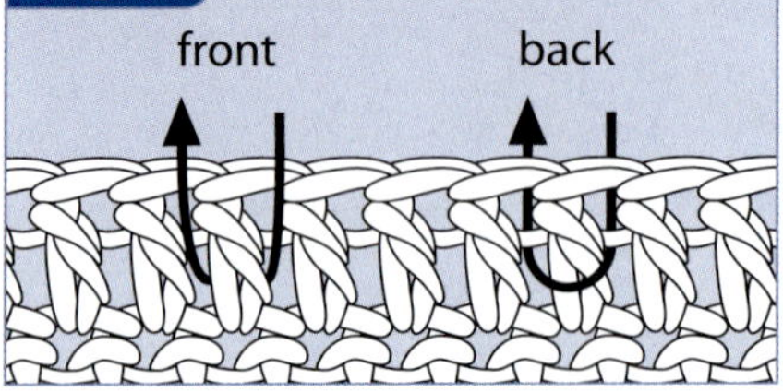

REVERSE SINGLE CROCHET

(abbreviated reverse sc)

Working from **left** to **right**, ★ insert hook in st to right of hook ***(Fig. 4a)***, YO and draw through, under and to left of loop on hook (2 loops on hook) ***(Fig. 4b)***, YO and draw through both loops on hook ***(Fig. 4c)*** **(reverse sc made, *Fig. 4d*)**; repeat from ★ around.

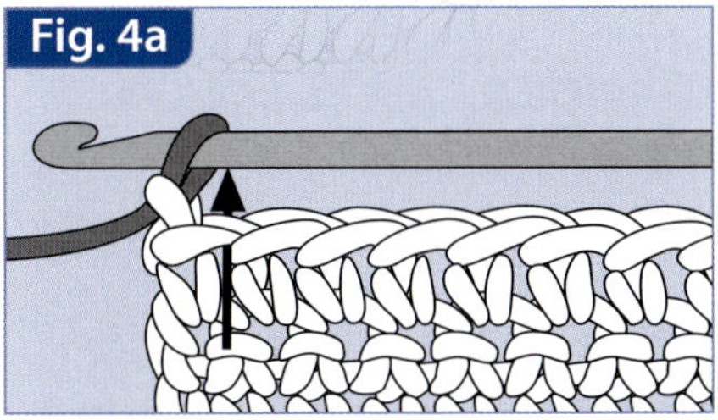
Fig. 4a

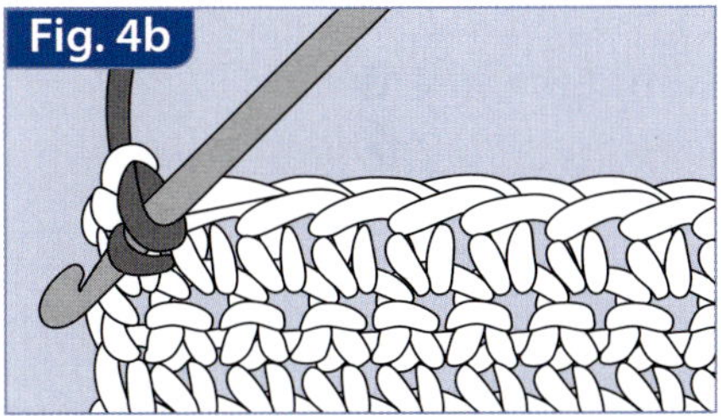
Fig. 4b

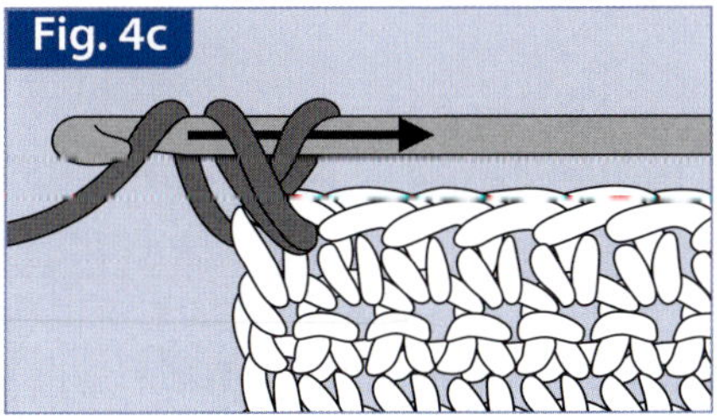
Fig. 4c

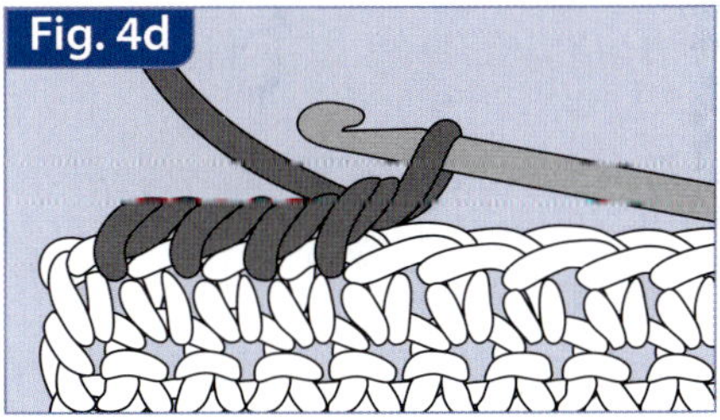
Fig. 4d

YARN INFORMATION

Each project in this book was made using Medium Weight Yarn. Any brand of Medium Weight Yarn may be used. It is best to refer to the yardage/meters when determining how many balls or skeins to purchase. Remember, to arrive at the finished size, it is the GAUGE/TENSION that is important, not the brand of yarn. For your convenience, listed below are the specific yarns used to create our photography models. Because yarn manufacturers make frequent changes in their product lines, you may sometimes find it necessary to use a substitute yarn or to search for the discontinued product at alternate suppliers (locally or online).

CABLED HANDBAG
Lion Brand® Heartland®
Dk Green - #180 Kings Canyon
Lt Green - #173 Everglades

MESSENGER BAG
Lily® Sugar'n Cream®
#18743 Hot Blue

BRAIDED TABLET COVER
Red Heart® With Love®
#1401 Pewter

BRAIDED COLUMNS TABLET COVER
Bernat® Handicrafter® Cotton
#00052 Potpourri Ombre

DIAMONDS & CABLES BACKPACK
Lily® Sugar'n Cream®
#18046 Rose Pink

RIBBED & CABLED PHONE COZY
Red Heart® Boutique Unforgettable®
#3977 Sunrise

PETITE SHOULDER BAG
Red Heart® Boutique Midnight®
#9803 Borealis

BEADED BROOMSTICK LACE BACKPACK
Bernat® Handicrafter® Cotton
#00001 White

Production Team: Writer/Instructional Editor - Sarah J. Green; Editorial Writer - Susan Frantz Wiles; Senior Graphic Artist - Lora Puls; Photo Stylist - Lori Wenger; and Photographer - Jason Masters.